This I Know About Life

Copyright © 2018 Jessie Jerome McNeil. All rights reserved. This book may not be reproduced in whole or in part without written permission from the publisher, except by a reviewer who may quote brief passages in a review; nor may any part of this book be reproduced, stored in retrieval system, or transmitted in any form or by any means, electronic, mechanical, photocopying, recording, or other, without written permission from the publisher.

ISBN-13: 978-0-9791560-2-1 (Paperback Edition)
978-0-9792560-9-0 (eBook Edition)

All photographs are owned by the author unless otherwise credited
Book design by Ersula Odom

Printed and bound in USA
First Printing December 2018

Published by Sula Too LLC
5508 N 50th St, Suite 16A
Tampa FL 33610
www.sulatoo.com

A Book of Call to Action Quotes

This I Know About Life

The first book in the:
"Once You Know
You Can't Un-know"
Series

Jessie J McNeil

Sula Too LLC Publishing

Tampa, Florida

*To Request
Volume Pricing*

Or

*To Book Jessie J McNeil
for your next event*

*Visit
www.jessiejmcneil.com*

Dedication

Giving all glory to my Father in Heaven.

My profound thanks to my beautiful wife for continuously pushing me to greatness and allowing me to grow as our Father ordained it in my life.

To my terrific kids who I can just imagine what wonderful adults you are destined to become.

To my family for seeing the importance of life through quotes.

To my friends who have allowed me to grow and learn with them, as well, in their journey.

To everyone who shared their knowledge and expertise, to you all, I extend my deep appreciation. I am living, This I Know About Life.

Jessie J McNeil

Table of Contents

Be Humble	3
It's Your Move	9
Embrace Your Inner Toughness	21
Cultivate Your Best You	33
Be A Hero	49
Engage Your Higher Power	57

@jessiejmcneil

This I Know - About Life

@jessiejmcneil

Jessie J McNeil

Be Humble

@jessiejmcneil

This I Know - About Life

~ 1 ~

All your assurances

sit in the corner of your heart.

@jessiejmcneil

Jessie J McNeil

~2~

***Love is like
living without glasses.***

***You must see things
clearly.***

@jessiejmcneil

This I Know - About Life

~3~

***Sometimes
you must take
your attitude down***

***to get out of some
situations.***

***Never allow yourself to be
taken out of character.***

@jessiejmcneil

Jessie J McNeil

@jessiejmcneil

This I Know - About Life

@jessiejmcneil

Jessie J McNeil

It's Your Move

@jessiejmcneil

This I Know - About Life

~4~

*Sometimes in life,
your words
have very little value.*

*At that point
you must
prophesy
with your actions.*

@jessiejmcneil

Jessie J McNeil

~5~

*For you to continue
to be great
you must attack your
fears.*

*Attack them
even though you may
fail.*

*Attack them for
when you overcome that
fear,
all other fears
will begin to tremble.*

@jessiejmcneil

This I Know - About Life

~6~

*How long
are you going to
hold on to a
dysfunctional system
and
allow life to pass you by?*

@jessiejmcneil

This I Know - About Life

~8~

You will always live in confusion

If you refuse to figure it out.

@jessiejmcneil

Jessie J McNeil

~9~

*The less room
you have
for the things
that are not
helping you grow,*

*The more room
You will have
to create a dynasty.*

@jessiejmcneil

This I Know - About Life

~10~

Be your own biggest supporter.

When you're down, raise yourself up.

When you're up, give yourself enough praise to keep going.

@jessiejmcneil

Jessie J McNeil

~11~

*I used to
walk and talk
like I knew
what I was doing.*

*Now, I walk and talk
because
I know why
I'm doing it.*

*Know
Your
WHY.*

@jessiejmcneil

This I Know - About Life

~12~

Take breaks and sometimes even pause,

But never stop.

@jessiejmcneil

Jessie J McNeil

Embrace Your Inner Toughness

@jessiejmcneil

This I Know - About Life

~13~

***You won't know
how strong you are***

***until you have
no other choice***

but to be strong.

@jessiejmcneil

Jessie J McNeil

~14~

***Nail down
your strengths,***

***So, you can discover
your passions.***

@jessiejmcneil

This I Know - About Life

~15~

***Many of us
look around
to find someone
to help us solve a
problem.***

***If you would like to
solve a problem***

***take your hand
and point to yourself.***

@jessiejmcneil

Jessie J McNeil

~16~

Life would take you places,

but if you allow that urge to drown you,

you will still live but unseen.

@jessiejmcneil

This I Know - About Life

~17~

Don't keep yourself

locked in
an unlocked room

because of fear.

@jessiejmcneil

Jessie J McNeil

~18~

Don't allow everything that's hurting you now,

change the song you dance to in the future.

@jessiejmcneil

This I Know - About Life

~19~

When you feel like you're at your lowest point and you don't want to push,

that's when you push your hardest.

@jessiejmcneil

Jessie J McNeil

~20~

***Channel
your pain

into determination.***

@jessiejmcneil

This I Know - About Life

~21~

You will fall.

Get up

You will fall again,
Get up
again.

Get up again.

Until you reach
your desire destination.

@jessiejmcneil

Jessie J McNeil

Cultivate Your Best You

@jessiejmcneil

This I Know - About Life

~22~

I love being me.

The best me

that you see.

@jessiejmcneil

Jessie J McNeil

~23~

When your perspective changes,

your reality changes.

@jessiejmcneil

This I Know - About Life

~24~

You are priceless.

You are valuable.

There's no money on earth that can buy you.

God spent the ultimate price.

He spent his blood which was invaluable.

@jessiejmcneil

Jessie J McNeil

~25~

When you connect with someone,

make sure that person is connected with you as well.

The power of attachment can help you or destroy you.

Attach wisely.

@jessiejmcneil

This I Know - About Life

~26~

Which do you feel more comfortable drinking

A glass of pure water clean water

or a glass of cloudy muggy water?

Make your life that way from your choices transparent.

@jessiejmcneil

Jessie J McNeil

~27~

*I woke up ready
to WIN.*

*I can .
I will.
Watch me.*

@jessiejmcneil

This I Know - About Life

~28~

*When you walk
by faith,
sometimes
you must walk it
alone.*

*Don't allow anyone to
take you off
your journey.*

@jessiejmcneil

Jessie J McNeil

~29~

***When light enters a
room,
it destroys darkness.***

***Be your own light
don't wait
for someone else
to be it.***

@jessiejmcneil

This I Know - About Life

~30~

***The only limitations
on your life is
the cap you placed on it.***

***Go pass
what you don't know
and learn something new
daily.***

@jessiejmcneil

Jessie J McNeil

~31~

***Sometimes in life
you need to go
a little further
than expected
to get to where you need to
be.***

***Stop putting periods
where you should
be placing commas
and complete all that you
were created to do.***

@jessiejmcneil

This I Know - About Life

~32~

Your hope is connected to your tomorrow so, if you have no hope, you'll always be trapped in your today.

Always hope for the better.

@jessiejmcneil

Jessie J McNeil

~33~

You are the best you, so why are you doubting yourself.

Don't be scared to be you.

You are a one and only you.

What's for you, is only for you.

@jessiejmcneil

This I Know - About Life

~34~

*Walk,
Speak, and
Succeed.*

*You will drive
Your own path
To your success.*

@jessiejmcneil

@jessiejmcneil

This I Know - About Life

@jessiejmcneil

Jessie J McNeil

Be A Hero

@jessiejmcneil

This I Know - About Life

~35~

***The child in you
shall grow up
with your children,***

***teaching them the mistakes
you made as a child.***

@jessiejmcneil

Jessie J McNeil

~36~

When a child suffers,

our future suffers.

@jessiejmcneil

This I Know - About Life

~37~

All fathers must follow their TUSK system.

***Teach
Understand
Speak and
Kiss.***

@jessiejmcneil

Jessie J McNeil

~38~

*Don't be so caught up
where you can't fulfill
the chance to fill
someone else.*

*Be intentional
be available
be fearless.*

SOMEONE
*may need you,
now.*

Be there.

@jessiejmcneil

This I Know - About Life

~39~

*Activate your
little kid power
to move that
gigantic mountain.*

You can do it.

@jessiejmcneil

Jessie J McNeil

~40~

*Confront your now
and
dance with your future.*

You are responsible for that.

@jessiejmcneil

Jessie J McNeil

Engage Your Higher Power

@jessiejmcneil

This I Know - About Life

~41~

***Stop wanting with
your arms stretched
facing east and west
and
palms facing north.***

***Start wanting
with your arms
at 10 and 2 above
and
all your desires
will be activated.***

@jessiejmcneil

Jessie J McNeil

~42~

***Don't be fearful
of the storm
or the circumstance,***

trust God,

***for his timing is
perfect.***

@jessiejmcneil

This I Know - About Life

~43~

Hanged.
Bled.
Died.

All for me.

I know my worth.
Do You?

@jessiejmcneil

Jessie J McNeil

~44~

***So,
know that you
are so expensive,***

***you are valuable
and important.***

@jessiejmcneil

This I Know - About Life

~45~

***Karma stole
the gift from God,***

Jesus saved us first.

@jessiejmcneil

Jessie J McNeil

~46~

Following him,
That's our
responsibility.

Molding us, that's his.

Thank you, Father.

@jessiejmcneil

This I Know - About Life

~47~

***You do your part,
God will do his.***

Don't confuse the two.

@jessiejmcneil

Jessie J McNeil

~48~

*You didn't
have to do it Lord,*

*but you did it
anyways.*

*The blessings
he blessed me with
he will bless you with.*

Have faith.

@jessiejmcneil

This I Know - About Life

~49~

*You never know
what may happen next.*

*Position yourself
for the blessings
you are praying for,*

*so when the blessings come
you're ready for them.*

*In the time in between,
keep believing that it will
happen.*

@jessiejmcneil

Jessie J McNeil

~50~

***Allow fire to be
a purifying agent
in your life.***

When under it,

***kneel down
to your truth.***

@jessiejmcneil

This I Know - About Life

~51~

**Don't hide
in your pride**

because

**your truth will be
overlooked.**

@jessiejmcneil

Jessie J McNeil

~52~

***Other people
may have more talent,***

***more education
or experience,***

***but God's favor
can cause
you to go places
you can own.***

@jessiejmcneil

Jessie J. McNeil is a Generational Chain Breaker and the oldest of three children. Growing up at times was a challenge, however for every problem that arose, there was a solution and a lesson. Jessie is a graduate of Hillsborough High School and pursuing an education degree from the University of South Florida.

With over 14 plus years of business leadership, Jessie has made a remarkable impression in business and his community. Mr. McNeil wears many hats from Entrepreneur to Founder. One of his many desires is to help

@jessiejmcneil

Jessie J McNeil

the younger generation in realizing their true potential through education and developing healthy business practices, while advancing in leadership to further their education.

Jessie is currently active in the community. Some of his passions are feeding and clothing the homeless, volunteering with back-to-school drives, speaking engagements, motivating others and giving back to the community. As an active member in church, Jessie believes there is always work to be done in the Kingdom of God, he certainly loves and enjoys serving God, his family and people.

Jessie does not take where he is today lightly and attributes a lot of his success to his wonderful wife who strongly believes in doing above and beyond the status quo. Jessie is the husband to one wife and 3 beautiful children. Therefore, while he has breath in his body he will continue to serve God, his family and community. He vows to continue being a voice to the voiceless, a father to the fatherless and seek to show compassion, encouragement and to empower every person he meets. His message is clear "Once you know, you can't unknow".

Jessie, is writing and will publish several books. His determination and humble attitude drives him to success with his one of his motto's that "Failure isn't an option, it's a choice."

@jessiejmcneil

www.ingramcontent.com/pod-product-compliance
Lightning Source LLC
Chambersburg PA
CBHW050606300426
44112CB00013B/2095